KU-719-707

DUDLEY SCHOOLS
LIBRARY SERVICE

Schools Library and Information Services
S00000678615

MEDIEVAL LIVES

Knight

MOIRA BUTTERFIELD

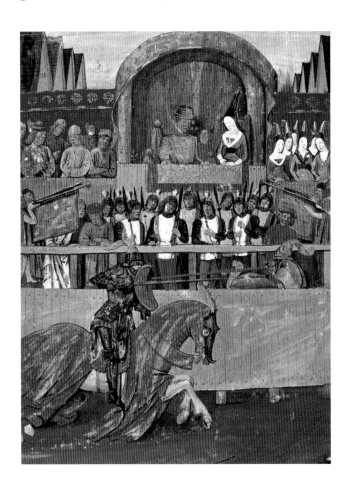

FRANKLIN WATTS
LONDON•SYDNEY

First published in 2008 by Franklin Watts

Copyright © Franklin Watts 2008
Artwork copyright © Gillian Clements 2008

Franklin Watts
338 Euston Road
London NW1 3BH

Franklin Watts Australia
Level 17/207 Kent Street
Sydney, NSW 2000

All rights reserved.

A CIP catalogue record for this book is available
from the British Library.

Dewey number: 940.1

SUD...... LIBRARIES

678615   SCH
J940.1

ISBN 978 0 7496 7738 1

Printed in China

Franklin Watts is a division of Hachette Children's
Books, an Hachette Livre UK company.

Artwork: Gillian Clements
Editor: Sarah Ridley
Editor in chief: John C. Miles
Designer: Simon Borrough
Art director: Jonathan Hair
Picture research: Diana Morris

Picture credits:

ArquBiblioteca d'Ajuda Lisbon/ Gianni Dagli Orti/The Art Archive: 11. Biblioteca Monasterio del Escorial Madrid/Bridgeman Art Library:36. Biblioteca Nazionale Marciana Venice/Alfredo Dagli Orti/The Art Archive: 19. Biblioteca Nazionale Marciana Venice/Gianni Dagli Orti/The Art Archive: 29, 40. Bibliothèque des Arts Décoratifs Paris/Gianni Dagli Orti/The Art Archive: 17b. Bibliothèque Nationale Paris/The Art Archive: front cover, 27, 32, 33. British Library London/The Art Archive: 12, 35, 37, 39. Cabinet des Estampes Strasbourg/Gianni Dagli Orti/The Art Archive: 9. Canterbury Cathedral/Alfredo Dagli Orti/The Art Archive: 34. Mary Evans Picture Library: 18.Andrew Fox/Corbis: 14, 17t. Paul Hutley/Eye Ubiquitous/Corbis: 20. Jarrold Publishing/The Art Archive: 38. JFB/The Art Archive: 21. Martin Jones/Corbis: 10. Private Collection/Marc Charmet /The Art Archive: 24. Real Biblioteca de lo Escorial/Gianni Dagli Orti/The Art Archive: 5, 22. Statsbibliothek Nuremberg/Bridgeman Art Library: 31. University Library Heidelberg/Gianni Dagli Orti/The Art Archive: 13.V & A Museum London/Eileen Tweedy/The Art Archive: 15.

Every attempt has been made to clear copyright. Should there be any inadvertent omission please apply to the publisher for rectification.

CONTENTS

ALL ABOUT KNIGHTS

T he medieval period of European history runs from about 1000 to 1500. This was the era of the knights and a time of wars and crusades. In legend knights are always brave fighters, jousting champions and men of honour. But were real knights anything like the ones we imagine in films and stories? This book follows the imaginary life of a knight in the 1300s but is based on true facts about the real knights of medieval Europe.

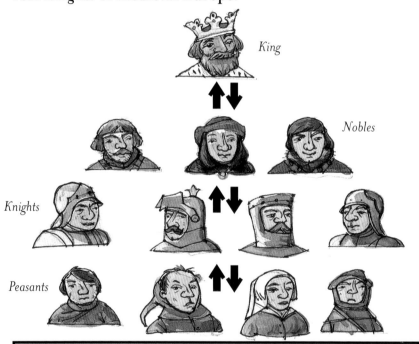

King

Nobles

Knights

Peasants

The ideal knight

The English poet Geoffrey Chaucer describes an ideal knight in his 14th century book *The Canterbury Tales*. This quote has been translated from the original into modern English:

❖ *There was a knight, a most distinguished man,*
Who from the day on which he first began
To ride abroad had followed chivalry,
Truth, honour, generousness and courtesy.
He had done nobly in his sovereign's war
And ridden into battle, no man more. ❖

Feudal society

Medieval society was feudal, being made up of different people linked together by a network of agreements. At the top was the king who owned all the land. Then came the important nobles, who were given big areas of land by the king in return for service, which meant fighting for him when required. When the king needed them to fight, they had to bring along a number of men, including their knights. A noble could grant a knight a manor, an estate with some houses and land, in return for fighting a certain number of days a year. The knight swore 'fealty' (loyalty) to his lord (the noble) and became his 'vassal', his sworn servant. The knight, in turn, rented his land out to tenants (mostly peasants) in return for them farming it and paying him with food or money.

Fighting times

The rules of service for knights changed through the centuries. At first they were expected to fight for their lord for 40 days a year, for free. After the 40 days were up, they got paid. Later on, some knights became paid professionals, full-time fighters who rarely returned home. Knights could pay to avoid fighting, if they preferred, and were even allowed to pass on the cost of this to their tenants.

During medieval times knights were to be found in Europe, where there were four main kingdoms – France, Spain, England and the Holy Roman Empire (including parts of central Europe, Germany and Italy). Wales, Northern Ireland and Scotland were not yet fully under English control.

Pictures such as this one from the 1800s have contributed to the romanticised – and inaccurate – ideas that people have about knights.

The knight

The knight whose life this book will follow is born in 1319. He comes from a long line of knights, armed horsemen. His family originally came over to England from Normandy, France in 1066, with William the Conqueror's invading army. The family were given English land in return for fighting on the winning side. As a result, many knights have French-sounding surnames. In the 1300s there are about 6,000 knights in England.

A FUTURE KNIGHT IS BORN

The knight's family already has one son who, because he is the eldest male child, will one day inherit all his father's land. They hope for a second son although he will have to claim some land for himself when he is older, by fighting well and impressing a noble. Altogether, the lady of the manor will give birth to four boys and four girls but only a couple will survive past childhood.

Home sweet home

The manor-house where the knight's family lives is like a mini castle. It has a gatehouse and walls around it. Inside the walls are a courtyard, kitchen block, stables and a bigger building where the Great Hall, the large main room, is to be found. In the Great Hall the knight meets

Medieval facts

In medieval times a child was thought to be an infant until the age of seven and a child until the age of 14. If a knight died when his heir was small, the baby could be sent by the lord to the household of a guardian, and the mother might have to pay to get her child back.

Some medieval manor-houses, such as Ightham Mote in Kent, had a water-filled moat to protect the inhabitants.

visitors, the family eats and the servants sleep in corners. Up above is the solar, which is the private family area.

There is a village on the manor lands and some of the village women have heard that the lady of the manor is in labour. They are now in the solar of the manor-house to help at the birth. Soon the news of the birth of a baby boy is announced, and the villagers are pleased. Their lord, the knight, is good to them but, if he died without an heir, *his* lord could give the estate to a stranger. With two sons in the family, this becomes less likely.

A medieval baby

The new baby is baptised on the day of his birth, given his name and immersed in the chapel font three times. It is done as soon as he is born, in case he doesn't survive long. If he died unbaptised the Church says he wouldn't go to heaven. His mother does not feed him herself but finds him a wet-nurse, a woman of the village who has recently given birth. She will breast-feed the baby for about 18 months, until he is strong. For now, he is swaddled (wrapped

tightly) for most of the time in bandages, so he won't injure himself flailing around. It is also said that this will help his limbs to grow straight.

The retired knight

The baby's father is in his late 30s. His fighting days as a knight are over, and now he has retired to look after his estate, which is made up of the land his family has held for many years as well as the land that his wife's family gave them when they married. The baby's father owes fealty (fighting service) to the local lord, who has rights over this knight's family. The lord can tell the knight's children who

A medieval baby, tightly wrapped, or swaddled, in bandages.

Baptism

In 1302 Pope Boniface declares that humans can only go to heaven if they are Catholic.
❖ *It is necessary to salvation that every human creature be subject to the Roman pontiff.* ❖

to marry, and if their father dies when they are young he might take all the money (rents and so forth) generated by the dead knight's lands, until the oldest child is old enough to inherit.

At the age of seven the young boy is sent away from home to live in the household of another knight. He is going to spend the next few years being a 'page'. His parents choose a knight who lives in a manor like their own, not too far away. If they were important nobles, their son would have gone to the king's court as a page.

Medieval facts

In the 1300s, tales of King Arthur's knights became very popular. The Church and the king encouraged these stories in the hope that they would prompt knights to be brave and chivalrous, rather than violent troublemakers.

Learning from ladies

The young page starts his new life under the direction of the ladies in his new home. They teach him courtly manners and social skills, such as dancing and reciting poetry. He learns something of music and of the Bible, too. As a knight he will be expected to cope well if he finds himself in somebody's court, with ladies to entertain. At dinner he learns how to carve the meat and serve a meal to his lord. In this way he is learning a lesson of allegiance, serving those above him.

A 14th-century page shows off his courtly manners in front of a group of noble ladies.

Fighting and writing

The young page also begins to learn the skills he will need to be a fighting knight. He goes hunting with the adults, learning to ride and to shoot arrows accurately. He is lucky because there is a chaplain in the household, a priest who teaches him some Latin and writing, using a feather quill on parchment made from goatskin. Most people in England cannot read or write, so he will have an advantage over them.

While he is at the knight's house he hears of trouble at the royal court. In 1327 news reaches them that Edward II has been murdered by his wife Isabella and her lover, Mortimer. In 1330 Edward II's son, Edward III, becomes old enough to take the throne. He imprisons Isabella and has Mortimer killed. These are uncertain times for knights, who must stay friendly with whomever is in power, so as not to lose their home and lands.

Stern words from Spanish writer Philip of Novara in the 13th century:

❖ *Few children perish from excess of severity but many from being permitted too much.* ❖

A page holds the bridle of a German knight's horse in this 14th-century painting.

A busy page

The page does not have a room of his own in the manor-house; he sleeps in the Great Hall, in a warm corner near the fire. He is allowed to go home for holidays, birthdays and special holy days. When he isn't learning he is kept busy with chores indoors and out. He must lay the table for meals, light fires, work in the garden and look after animals. All this will prepare him for a time when he might rule an estate of his own. He will have some understanding of how to run it, and what work is needed.

BECOMING A SQUIRE

When he is 14, the page's parents watch their son receive a simple sword in a ceremony confirming him as a squire. He swears an oath of fealty, of service, to the knight in whose household he lives. He is now expected to be that knight's personal servant in battle.

Serious training

Now the young knight-to-be's training begins in earnest. He learns to aim his lance at the quintain, a swinging wooden arm with a shield on one side and a heavy sack on the other. If he fails to hit the shield full-on, the sack will swing round and knock him on the back of the head! He also practises aiming his lance through metal rings hanging in the trees.

He learns to ride superbly, controlling the horse with his knees and feet so that his hands are free to hold weapons. The saddle he uses is shaped high at the front and back to help him stay on. He trains with two other squires and sometimes has a mock sword-fight with them, using wooden swords.

The squire

Geoffrey Chaucer wrote a description of a squire in his *Canterbury Tales*, written in the 14th century. This version has been translated into modern English:

❖ *Short was his gown, the sleeves were long and wide;*
He knew the way to sit a horse and ride.
He could make songs and poems and recite,
Knew how to joust and dance, to draw and write. ❖

A modern version of a quintain. If the young squire misses the centre of the shield, a heavy ball swings around and hits him.

Medieval facts

Groups of squires sometimes behaved very badly when they got together, occasionally getting out of control and having mass fights at events such as tournaments.

A smartly dressed squire shows off his riding skills – from a manuscript painting.

Body-building medieval-style

The squire works at building up his strength, so he will be strong enough to wear heavy chain mail armour and mount a horse while wearing it. He tries to make himself stronger using a well-known squire's trick, sewing dirt into the pockets and hems of his clothing to make it feel heavier. He becomes good at vaulting over his horse while wearing chain mail, and he rides hard whilst out hunting, leaping over ditches and hedges. He and the other squires are competitive, trying to outdo each other in showing off their knightly skills.

The ideal knight

As a squire, he learns about the code of chivalry, a list of rules set out by the Catholic Church explaining what it means to be a good and noble knight. The ideal knight is supposed to protect the Church, women and children, the poor and the weak. On the battlefield he is supposed to play fair, always accepting the surrender of an enemy knight and not killing an unarmed opponent. In reality, though, knights often behave badly. Some are extremely violent, and rob whoever they come across. The code is designed to try to keep the violent tendencies of knights in check.

A SQUIRE GOES FORTH

The squire acts as his lord's – his knight's – personal servant. He must go with him when he is called to do battle. In 1335, when the squire is 16, his lord's lord (the earl) calls upon his knights to help him put down a rebellion. The earl owes an obligation to the king to bring along knights, squires, archers and men-at-arms (other troops, such as foot soldiers).

A knight in costume

An anonymous medieval poet described a knight in armour as:
❖ *… a terrible worm in an iron cocoon.* ❖

On the journey

Our squire sets out with one of his fellow squires to accompany the knight, their lord. They ride ahead, loaded down with baggage and leading spare horses. Before the trip, they clean the knight's armour in a barrel filled with vinegar and sand.

Along the way, the squires care for the horses and make sure all the equipment is safe. They act almost as butlers for the knight, folding his clothes, finding accommodation and even tidying his hair for him. They help him to put on his armour and mount his horse.

All is ready

On route, they are involved in a skirmish, a small-scale conflict with a band of rebels. Our squire quickly hands over the knight's shield. The other young squire stays well behind the fighting, holding on to the spare horses. The knight crosses himself before he joins the fight, making the sign of the cross on his chest to ask for God's protection and mercy. Then he and his fellow knights ride at the enemy, while the squires watch anxiously. If the rebels get the upper hand the squires will have to fight for their lives.

A knight rides forth with his squire in attendance.

Medieval facts

The word 'squire' comes from a French word, *ecuyer*, meaning a 'shield-bearer'. Holding a knight's shield is part of the squire's duty before a battle.

A squire in battle

If their knight is wounded during the fight the squires must try to get him off the battlefield out of danger. It is no easy job, as a knight's armour weighs him down, and the squires could be attacked by the enemy. Luckily for them, their knight is unharmed, but it is a close-fought skirmish and, though the squire has trained nearly all his life for fighting, his first taste of being at a real fight is frightening. His experience of attending battles as a squire is designed to help him cope when he finally becomes a knight.

The squire's knight wears chain mail and carries a heavy sword, as in this modern reconstruction.

A procession of knights and squires, weary from travel, enter the safety of a castle. From a 15th-century painting.

BECOMING A KNIGHT

At the age of 18 our squire is judged ready to become a knight. He has already seen battle, and he proved brave and dependable. His lord is going to 'dub' him – give him a knighthood in a special ceremony. Only a knight can dub another knight.

Preparing for the ceremony

The squire's parents are going to attend the ceremony, the most important day of their son's life so far. He must prepare for it by fasting (not eating) for two days. His hair is cut short and he takes a bath to symbolically wash away his sins. Baths are an unusual occurrence – he

The kind knight

Chrétien de Troyes, a 12th century French writer, stated:
❖ *A knight must be merciful without wickedness, friendly and not treacherous, kind towards the suffering, and honest.* ❖

usually washes with water from a well. Before the day of the ceremony he goes to the chapel and keeps a vigil, which means he prays to God through the whole night, his sword laid on the altar.

Dressing for the part

On the special day, he is given ceremonial clothes to remind him of his religious duties as a knight. He is dressed in a belt and robe of white, to symbolise cleanliness. His red cloak is to remind him of his duty to shed blood in the defence of God. His brown stockings represent the earth he will one day return to when he dies. He is given shiny spurs to ensure he is swift at doing God's commands. The two edges of his sword represent justice and loyalty, and the crosspiece at the top symbolises the holy cross.

A romanticised 19th-century picture of a squire keeping a vigil on the night before his dubbing ceremony.

If a squire showed great bravery on the battlefield, he might be dubbed there and then. Not only was this a great honour but also much cheaper than a ceremony at home! A knight could only surrender to another knight during battle so occasionally, if a squire took a knight prisoner, the enemy knight would have to dub the squire on the spot, so that the knight could surrender properly.

Arise, knight!

The squire kneels before his lord, the knight, with his head bowed. The knight draws his own sword, holds it high above the squire's head and calls out his name. He makes a speech calling upon the squire to defend the weak, the poor and the Church, and to obey his lord and king. Then he taps the squire on each shoulder with the flat of the sword. These are the only blows that the young man is expected to receive from now on, without retaliating. He is now a knight.

Afterwards there is a celebration feast. The ceremony is expensive for the new knight's family so their tenants will be asked to pay some of the cost of making this second son a knight. If they were from a grand family, the young man might have been knighted at court, along with other squires. Then there would have been a tournament and days of partying.

A king creates a new knight in this 14th-century manuscript painting.

INVITATION TO THE CASTLE

Now that he has been knighted, the young knight is invited to attend a jousting tournament at the Earl of Oxford's castle. Without the earl's goodwill, the young knight will never hold any land. He hopes to impress the earl and get a place in his service, as a knight in his entourage, helping to guard the castle.

Hedingham Castle, the seat of the Earl of Oxford, is the most perfectly preserved Norman castle in the UK. This photo shows the keep.

The castle stronghold

The Earl of Oxford's castle is built with stone walls over 3.5 m thick. Not only do they keep out the cold, but they make for a strong defence. The stronghold was first built in Norman times, when the family came over with William the Conquerer. The family name, de Vere, represents their French background. The great castle can be seen from the countryside around, reminding the local people who is in charge. As he approaches, the young knight can see guards up on the ramparts, armed with arrows. There is a moat, a portcullis and a drawbridge to let friends in but keep enemies out.

Castle building

The chronicler Ordericus describes what happened to the unfortunate architect of Castle Ivri, in Normandy, during the late 11th century:

❖ *This is the famous castle of great size and strongly fortified which was built by Alberede wife of Ralph, Count of Bayeux. It is said that Alberede, having completed this castle at vast expense, caused Lanfred, whose character as an architect transcended that of all other French architects of the time... to be beheaded that he might not erect a similar fortress anywhere else.*

Medieval facts

English nobles, such as earls and barons, spoke a form of French at this time, as their families originated in France. It was a mark of high class to speak French.

French people feasting in the 15th century. Servants on bended knee present drinking cups to the nobles.

At a feast, many courses are placed together on the table at the same time, and musicians play in the gallery.

Inside the walls

Within its walls the castle has several different buildings, such as the stables, a chapel, workshops and kitchens. The knight enters the keep, an imposing tall square building which is the heart of the castle. He passes the guardhouse on the ground floor and then goes through a corridor to the Great Hall, where the earl receives visitors. It is more magnificent than any Great Hall he has seen before. It has a giant stone arch, high windows and a fire blazing in a huge hearth. Shields and stag heads, the earl's hunting trophies, hang from the walls. The earl's family are plainly very wealthy, and so they must be in favour with the king, who could easily take all this away if he so wished.

A grand feast

The new knight is invited to a feast, and because he is a knight he no longer has to sit at the far end of the hall with the squires. But he feels ashamed as he is not wearing new clothes, because they are too expensive for him. His armour, too, is second-hand from his father, and not the latest style. He must start to accumulate money of his own by winning booty in war or by winning prizes at tournaments so that he can afford new clothes.

The feast is luxurious. The servants serve the guests with many different courses: dishes such as meat, fish, baked eggs and tarts. There is spiced wine and expensive sugar sweets.

JOUST!

The jousting tournament is the knight's chance to impress the earl with his fighting skills, and perhaps win some prize money. The risk is that he will be badly injured. The contest is to be held in the castle meadows, and it will go on for a few days until a winner is found. There is a sword-fighting contest on foot as well as a joust, but the young knight thinks his best chance is on horseback.

A lord and lady watch a joust in 15th-century France.

Rules of jousting

When jousting first began it was chaotic and very dangerous, but in the 1300s there are strict rules to control what goes on. First there is an official parade and knights must register with the judges (only knights are allowed to take part). During a contest two knights thunder towards each other on horseback, each carrying a lance tipped with a breakable point called a coronel. Points are awarded for hitting either the centre or the edge of a knight's shield, for breaking the point of a lance, and for unhorsing an opponent. After a few bouts between two knights, the scores are added up and the winner goes on to fight in the next round.

The jousting crowd

There are grandstands for the most important spectators, and the crowds have fun at sideshows and foodstalls. They cheer on their favourite fighters. Some of the jousters are well-known professional jousting knights who travel from tournament to tournament, making a living from winning prizes. The ladies of the castle pick their favourite knights and give them favours to wear, such as a scarf or a circlet of flowers. Nobody has heard of the young knight, so he has everything to prove. He does well, and at the feast after the tournament the earl congratulates him on his skill. He has made a very good start as a young knight.

Knights had another sport, too. They sometimes took part in *combats à plaisance*, 'combats for pleasure'. For fun, one group of knights might try to defend a spot such as a bridge or a hill, against another group of knights.

Jousting dangers

The young knight is unharmed, but other knights are not so lucky. They break bones and must get some medical care. They might be given a painkiller, a syrup made from the henbane plant mixed with alcohol, while their limb is set. The most dangerous outcome is for a knight to get trapped as he falls, and then get dragged along by his galloping horse. That might well lead to death or incurable injury. Injured knights must hope that their wounds do not become infected in the next few days, for that will lead to amputation or death.

Unfortunately, amputation is quite common after battles. A limb must be cut off as quickly as possible with a sharp sword. It is bound up to stop the bleeding and cauterised (burnt with something red hot) to try to seal it from infection. Sometimes wounds are stitched with a bone needle and thread made from animal intestines.

Some knights needed medical treatment after a tournament. Here a knight from Castille (now Spain), Don Pero Nino, receives treatment for a wounded leg. The hot iron was used to seal his wound:

❖ *They heated an iron… white hot. The surgeon feared to apply it, having pity for the pain it would cause. But Pero Nino, who was used to such work, took the glowing iron and himself moved it over his leg, from one end of his wound to the other.* ❖

Lances shatter on shields as jousting knights collide.

CALLED TO WAR

Now that he is a knight in the Earl of Oxford's retinue (his personal guard), the young knight lives in the castle, ready to guard it if necessary. When King Edward III calls upon the earl to help fight his enemy, the knight goes, too, as one of the fighting men the earl is expected to provide for the king's army.

War means profit

War is a chance for a knight to make some money. If he captures a noble prisoner he can demand a ransom from the family, before setting his hostage free. He might be awarded some land back home, or even in a conquered country, if he fights well. Knights who have already inherited lands come to fight, too, as part of their obligations to the earl. They can go home after their regulation 40 days service, but our knight stays on and gets paid a wage by the earl. If his commanders allow it, he will take plunder from towns he helps to conquer, and have it sent home and sold for cash.

A scene from the Hundred Years' War – Edward the Black Prince (centre right) takes King John II of France prisoner at the battle of Poitiers in 1356.

Medieval facts

In 1192 the English King Richard I was captured in Austria and a 'king's ransom' of 150,000 silver marks was demanded, worth millions in modern terms. Much of this money was raised by taxing the English people.

24

Hundred Years' War

Edward III of England had a claim to the French throne. He and his successors fought for this claim in battles and skirmishes stretching over many years. This long conflict is now called the Hundred Years' War. It lasted from 1337 to 1453.

Pillage and murder

The knight takes part in a tactic called the 'chevauchée'. He helps to raid enemy country, laying waste to crops and setting fire to farms and villages. The aim is to insult the knights whose land is ravaged, anger the foreign king and draw the enemy army out to fight. The English army will go home in winter, when conditions for fighting are too difficult, so they want to get on with fighting as soon as they can. Any food is seized to feed the invading army and peasants are murdered. It is a brutal tactic, not at all in keeping with the idea of merciful honourable knighthood set out in stories told to young pages and ladies back home.

Knights at sea

For the next few years the knight accompanies the earl to sieges and skirmishes abroad. He travels by boat, along with his horses and equipment, returning home each winter after successful fighting. He is on the earl's ship when it blows off course and is shipwrecked. The crew and passengers are lucky to survive, though the locals rob them of everything they have.

During a siege abroad, the king sends the earl home to get fresh horses and supplies. He returns with 200 ships but they meet the enemy fleet and are forced to fight them at sea. In a sea battle such as this, the opposing archers fight a duel of arrows (below), and then the knights draw their swords and fight the enemy on deck. The knight fights bravely and his side wins and captures enemy ships.

BATTLEFIELD TACTICS

The knight's commanders are the senior nobles in charge of the king's forces. They decide how battles are to be fought and sieges carried out. The king's son is a skilled commander and, when he is present, he takes command, leading them to great victories.

Fighting in the 14th century

Before the knight's time, if a big battle was to be fought, knights would line up with the other knights on horseback, in a closely-packed row. When given the order they would charge, thundering down on the enemy army, piercing as many as they could with their lances before drawing their swords and slashing this way and that. But now the English are starting to fight differently, because the English archers are becoming so skilled with longbows, a large form of bow and arrow. They can kill enemy knights from quite a distance. Now the English knights dismount and stand with the archers, beating off the oncoming enemy until the enemy forces are exhausted and depleted. Then the English knights mount up and chase after the weakened enemy, cutting them down.

The Battle of Crécy

The knight has heard how, at the Battle of Crécy in 1346, the English positioned themselves on a ridge of higher ground, to defend themselves against the French, who still fought in the traditional way. Despite the fact that the French forces far outnumbered the English, the French were in for a big shock.

The English knights stood with the archers. First, the French sent their crossbowmen forward, without their proper shields in place (the shields had not arrived in time but the French were impatient to fight). The crossbowmen were being cut down by the archers when the mounted French knights could wait no longer, and rode over their own unfortunate crossbowmen to attack the English. Wave after wave of French knights on horseback were slaughtered by the longbowmen. Any who got through had to fight the English knights. It was a tremendous victory.

Fighting on foot

All that sword-fighting training comes into its own when the knight fights on foot. It's hard for him to move freely in his armour, but enemy knights are in the same position. He looks for coats-of-arms – badges of identification – on the shields and surcoats (tunics) of other knights, so he can tell who is an enemy and who is on his side. He has a big broad sword that needs both hands to wield it. His technique is to raise it high and drive it downwards. If he were ever to look like losing, he would surrender and hope that he can raise his ransom, but this never happens to the knight, who is an outstanding fighter. Occasionally he sees knights running away from battle, and this leaves them in disgrace. After the battle, foot soldiers pick up piles of armour and any weapons they want.

A 15th-century depiction of the Battle of Crécy showing English forces (left) about to cross the River Somme.

Battle of Crécy

Le Morte d'Arthur, a book about King Arthur written by Sir Thomas Malory in 1485, includes a long, detailed and violent description of a medieval battle:

❖ *Then Brastias smote one of them on the helm, that it went to the teeth, and he rode to another, and smote him, that the arm flew into the field. Then he went to the third and smote him on the shoulder, that shoulder and arm flew in the field.* ❖

Medieval facts

Surrendering knights could not always rely on the chivalry of the opponent. If they had angered victorious enemy commanders by withstanding a long siege, they might be hanged.

DRESSED TO KILL

By now the knight has bought himself some up-to-date armour and a fine warhorse. Styles of armour change frequently through the years, but one thing is for sure – it is very expensive. It is handmade and designed to keep out arrows and take sword blows without splitting. The knight can now afford to have it made individually for him by a blacksmith.

All kinds of armour

The knight's armour consists of lots of different pieces, including gauntlets, padded underclothes, and a number of protective armour plates held together with rivets and leather straps. He wears a chain mail coat, made from interlocking iron rings. It is called a hauberk, and it has a chain mail hood. Under the mail hood is a padded cap called a coif, and over it a helmet with a visor. He also wears cloth stockings underneath chain mail stockings with leather soles. He wears a surcoat – a cloth tunic – over the top of the chain mail coat. All the many elements of the costume have names derived from medieval French.

Heraldry

The knight's surcoat and his shield are all marked with his coat-of-arms (so called because it is displayed on the surcoat). He has adapted his traditional family coat-of-arms, adding some new details for himself. Every knight has their own coat-of-arms, which is recorded by official heralds. Each one has its own specific colours,

This mounted knight has the fleur-de-lis emblazoned on his shield repeated on his horse's long coat, or caparison

geometric design and symbol, such as an animal or an object. It might have stripes and a French motto. The earl has a coat-of-arms made up of red and yellow quarters with a white star in the top left quarter. Everyone recognises it because the earl is such a famous and successful fighting noble.

Warhorses

Like all knights, the knight chooses warhorses that are fast and strong. They are called 'destriers', and they cost a lot of money. They, too, wear armour pieces and sometimes chain mail. They wear a long cloth coat called a caparison or trapper, marked with their knight's coat-of-arms. Destriers are not ridden except in battle, and the knight has other horses for everyday riding. His destrier has been trained up in mock battles and it knows how to charge, turn and stop, obeying the pressure of the knight's knees and sharp spurs.

Medieval facts

Towards the end of the 14th century the amount of armour worn by knights made them so heavy it became difficult for them to get up if they fell. There are stories of helpless fallen knights having bonfires built around them by cruel enemies, or even being rolled into rivers.

Knight in shining armour

A contemporary description of a knight's armour can be found in the 14th-century tale *Sir Gawain and the Green Knight* by an unknown author. This is a modern translation:

❖ *He had polished armour on arms and elbows,*
Glinting and fine, and gloves of metal,
And all the goodly gear to give help, whatever
Befell him;
With surcoat richly wrought,
Gold spurs attached in pride,
A silken sword-belt athwart.
And steadfast blade at his side. ❖

Heavily armoured mounted knights clash in this 14th-century manuscript illustration.

WEAPONS

The knight has trained to use a sword and a lance in battle. His sword is expensive, made by a skilled craftsman. To lose it or to break it would be a costly misfortune. When he first became a knight he was given one of his lord's swords, as a gift. As his wealth has grown, he has had a finer, more decorated sword made for himself. He never forgets to have it blessed on a church altar before he uses it in battle.

Medieval facts

Occasionally knights might fight as a team, standing back-to-back in a circle. This way their backs are protected and they can concentrate on the enemy in front of them.

A fine fighting sword

The sword is made from steel heated and beaten into shape. While it is hot, the soft metal is folded over and over many times to make it stronger. The swords of really rich nobles have precious jewels embedded in the hilt. The knight's sword is not that grand, but it is engraved with beautiful patterns, and it fits into a finely-decorated leather scabbard. He also has a dagger to use if he loses his sword in battle. The best dagger-fighting technique is to stab an opponent in the eye through the visor of his helmet, or through gaps in his armour.

Different swords and weapons

Fashions in sword shapes change regularly, and knights who come from abroad carry different-styled ones. Some are short and wide; others long and tapered. All have a cross-guard, a piece at the top to protect the knight's hand. Some knights fight with small axes rather than daggers. Foot soldiers have bigger axes, with a jabbing spike.

Medieval weaponry including a flail, sword, lance and axes.

The Knight's Tale

'The Knight's Tale', part of Geoffrey Chaucer's *Canterbury Tales*, includes a description of a battle. This version has been translated into modern English:

❖ *Up spring the spears to twenty foot in height,*
Out go the long-swords flashing silver bright,
Hewing the helmets as they shear and shred.
Out bursts the blood in streams of sternest red,
The mighty maces swing, the bones are bashed. ❖

Time to surrender

The knight's worst fear is to meet an enemy with a weapon that will break open his armour, such as a foot soldier with a mace, flail or hammer. A mace is a metal ball nailed onto a wooden shaft. A flail is a wooden shaft attached to a chain with an iron ball on the end. If a knight finds himself at the mercy of such a weapon, he knows the best thing to do is surrender.

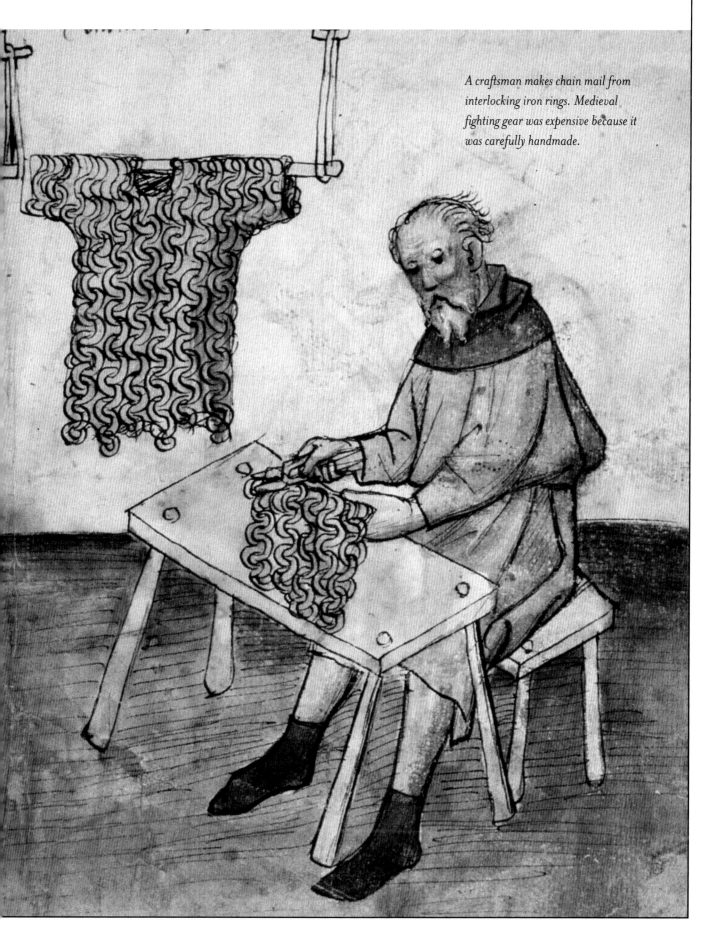

A craftsman makes chain mail from interlocking iron rings. Medieval fighting gear was expensive because it was carefully handmade.

SIEGE WARFARE

The knight is involved in a few sieges, surrounding any town that refuses to surrender. Most towns have high walls and try to keep any entrances protected by archers and fighting men. The townspeople inside hope to last until the enemy forces grow too tired and hungry to stay, or decide to go home for winter.

Siege equipment

Amongst the forces there are craftsmen who know how to build specialist equipment to help break into a town or castle. Wooden siege towers, like four-sided giant ladders, help troops reach the tops of walls, though they run the risk of being shot at from above. The knight has seen such siege towers set on fire by flaming arrows. Giant catapult machines called trebuchets fire missiles such as rocks to break down walls, and a battering ram can be used to try to break down any doors. It is fitted with a sharp iron tip and mounted on wheels, with a wooden roof over the top to protect its soldiers from missiles.

Mining or bribing?

The commanders decide on the best strategies to try to make a breech, a hole in a defensive wall where their troops can get through. One way to break into a town or castle is to dig a tunnel under its walls. As the miners dig, they shore up the tunnel walls with timbers. Once the tunnel is ready, the timbers are wrapped in pigskin and set alight. When they collapse, so does the tunnel, bringing down the wall above. However, digging takes a long time, and the people inside look out for signs of mining going on. They might dig a tunnel going the other way, and meet the enemy for an underground fight. However, the favourite and easiest way to break a siege is to bribe a traitor to open the gates from the inside.

This siege tower could be pushed right up to castle walls to attack the defenders.

Medieval facts

In 1203 knights got into the besieged Chateau Gaillard in France by crawling along the sewage trench. Once inside, the stinking knights, disguised as locals, lowered the drawbridge from the inside.

The violent behaviour of the English after their victory at the siege of Limoges, a town in France, in 1370, as chronicled by Froissart:

❖ *All who could be found were put to the sword, including many who were in no way to blame. I do not understand how they could not have failed to take pity on people who were too unimportant to have committed treason … More than three thousand men, women and children were dragged out to have their throats cut.* ❖

Surrender or die

If a besieged town or castle quickly surrenders, the people inside may be given quarter – mercy – by the victorious commanders. However, this is by no means certain, and the knight often sees troops running riot, with no-one able to control them. Men, women, children and priests may be put to the sword, and any enemy knights hanged. Even if the violence is controlled by the commanders, the people inside can expect to have anything of value taken. The troops move into people's homes, and a senior soldier is put in charge of the town. The knight plunders what he can and has it sent home by boat, to be sold.

English forces (left) storm the town of Caen in Normandy in 1346 – from an edition of Froissart's Chronicles.

PILGRIMAGE

Pilgrims were offered saintly relics by salesmen on their journey. These were usually described as blessed pieces of a saint's body, but were generally fakes, such as pieces of pig bone.

At the age of 36, the knight feels he has had enough of fighting. He is no longer expected to go abroad with the earl because he is too old, and so he is free to retire full-time to the estate he has been given by the earl for fighting bravely. But before he settles into country life, he wants to go on a pilgrimage.

A group of 14th-century pilgrims set off on their journey.

A holy journey

The knight travels to a holy shrine, a place connected to a saint who might hear his prayers and put in a good word for him in heaven. The journey is also the medieval version of a holiday. He chooses Canterbury and travels with his lively young squire and other pilgrims on a well-trodden route.

Pilgrimage

Geoffrey Chaucer describes a knight, once a heroic fighter but now done with battles, going on a pilgrimage in his *Canterbury Tales*. This version has been translated into modern English:

❖ *Speaking of his equipment, he possessed Fine horses, but he was not gaily dressed. He wore a fustian tunic stained and dark, With smudges where his armour had left mark.* ❖

By praying at Canterbury, pilgrims hope they will gain forgiveness for their sins. The knight also prays for the souls of those friends and family who died from the Black Death in the terrible years between 1348 to 1350. He is a survivor, but many people he knew from his father's estate died, and some from his own lands.

Fighting for religion

The knight remembers tales of his ancestors who fought religious wars in the Holy Land (now called the Middle East). For two hundred years after 1095, knights travelled to Jerusalem on crusades, to recapture the holy city from Islamic control. Crusader battles and sieges were fierce and bloody. There were terrible massacres and violent acts on both sides. From these crusades there grew a group of fighting monks called the Knights Templar. Now these Knights Templar have been destroyed by European monarchs who thought they were too powerful.

Religion

Everyone is religious in medieval England. The knight hears a Mass from a priest every day, and always makes a confession of his sins before battle, in case he dies. By confessing his sins, he believes they will be forgiven by God. Medieval England is a Roman Catholic country, like the rest of Europe at this time. The Pope is the religious leader, and he tries to get the monarchs to do what he regards as best for the Church. The Pope would like knights to go crusading again, but it's too expensive and there are battles to fight nearer home, so crusading is no longer a popular idea.

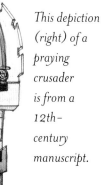

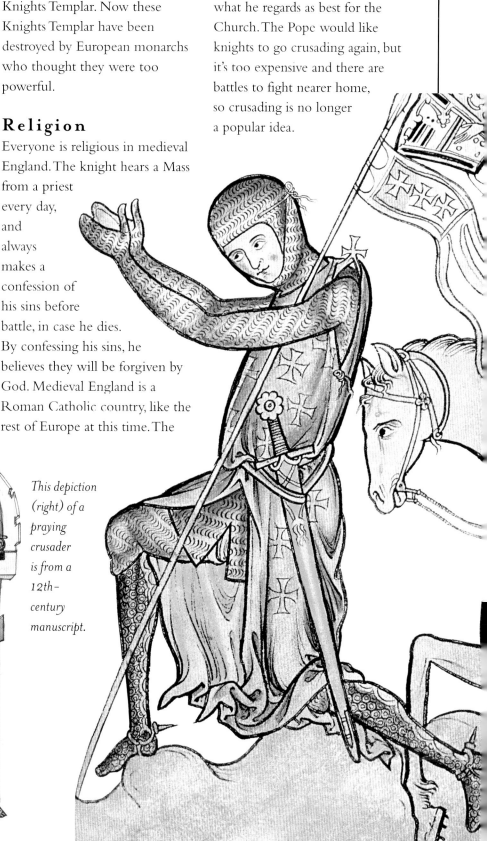

This depiction (right) of a praying crusader is from a 12th-century manuscript.

The knight returns to his estate, his fighting days over. His parents and the lord who trained him to be a knight have all died. His older brother has inherited the original family estate, paying an expensive 'relief', a very high tax of 100 shillings, to the earl to allow him to do so. The knight hasn't had to pay death duties in this way.

Medieval facts

Millers were notorious for cheating the peasants when they ground up their corn, lying about the quantity of flour they made. The knight was expected to keep a close check, to make sure his miller was honest.

The knight's wife

The knight married in his twenties, during a break between fighting seasons. He married quite late in life because he had no lands when he was young, so he was not a good prospect for a bride. By contrast, his older brother was betrothed (promised) as a seven-year-old child to another young child, and married her as soon as he was 14 and she was 12.

The earl chose a wife for the knight – the daughter of another one of his loyal knights.

The couple had no choice in the matter; they had to do what the earl wished, or risk his displeasure. The lady has looked after the knight's land and manor well every time he has gone away to fight. She has also given birth to four children, of whom a son and a daughter have survived past the age of five. Sadly, the others died of infections and diseases when they were babies. Now the knight returns home for good and takes over the running of the estates himself.

The daily round

The knight employs some servants to help him run his estate. He has a steward to help him sort out household matters, and he has a reeve to help him collect taxes due to him from the peasants. Every morning he 'makes the rounds', which means he rides around the estate with his steward, checking up on the state

Hunting with hawks was a sport enjoyed by many knights.

Peasants cut corn while the reeve supervises, from a 14th-century psalter.

of the farmland and the woods. He visits the mill, which he owns and rents to the miller. The miller grinds the corn grown by the local peasants, and the knight takes a daily percentage of the flour produced. It's the knight's duty to check up on the mill and on any shops he owns and rents out, such as the baker's, for instance. He wants to be sure they are clean and well-run. Otherwise he will start getting angry locals complaining to him.

Pleasures of the day

Most knights love to hunt, and it's a way of feeding the people who live in the manor-house. The knight has hunting dogs and he keeps hawks and falcons trained to hunt rabbits and small birds. He uses a bow and arrow to shoot deer and wild pigs in his woodlands. As the day draws to a close he spends time in his private quarters with his family, telling his children tales of his fighting days. Sometimes travelling entertainers visit, jugglers or a wandering minstrel singing songs of knightly legends and magical happenings.

Love of hunting

Below, a quote from the *Livre de Chasse*, by nobleman Gaston de Foix, a famous book on medieval hunting. Gaston himself died after a day out hunting in 1391.

❖ *All my life I have delighted especially in three things: one is arms, a second is love, and third is the chase.* ❖

KNIGHTLY DUTIES

At home the knight is the local judge as well as the tax-collector. He decides on disputes and chooses punishments. The tenants look to him to behave honourably and fairly. He also has a duty to offer them protection from any possible attack, and he trains the men in case they need to fight.

Medieval justice — the stocks pinned an offender's legs while villagers threw rubbish at them.

Knightly justice

The knight regularly holds court sessions in his Great Hall, where people come to lay complaints against others. These might vary from accusations of cheating or stealing, to more serious charges such as rape or murder. The most common grievances the knight deals with are disputes between neighbours over land or animals, poaching, shopkeepers cheating customers or someone complaining of a grave insult. He must judge on these and levy fines or physical punishment such as lashes, being placed in the village stocks, or hanging for a serious crime. Sometimes a jury help him decide on judgements.

Medieval facts

Occasionally a knight was attacked and beaten by angry peasants who thought his taxes were too high, and the knight's management of the estate wasn't good enough. That's why knights preferred to send the reeve to extract payment.

Collecting taxes

Every person who lives on the knight's land has an obligation (duty) to pay a 'quota', whether it be goods or money, to the knight. A farmer might pay in food, a shopkeeper in goods. A lowly peasant might work the lord's farmland for a few days and a peasant's wife might be sent to help out in the manor-house. The knight sends his reeve to collect taxes. The reeve takes a percentage of what he collects. If someone fails to pay they could be fined, physically punished or even face eviction.

Training up the locals

If the knight's lands are ever attacked, his tenants will expect him to give them shelter in his manor-house. He also trains the men to fight if needed. Every Sunday after church they gather in a meadow and he gets them to practise their archery. Sometimes he runs contests with prizes, to keep them interested and enthusiastic. He might hang up a straw dummy for them to hit, or mount a target on wheels and roll it along to see if they can hit it as it moves.

The reeve

Geoffrey Chaucer describes a canny tax-collecting reeve in *The Canterbury Tales*. This version is translated into modern English:

❖ *No bailiff, serf or herdsman dared to kick.*
He knew their dodges, knew their every trick. ❖

If the knight's manor was attacked, he was bound to shelter peasants such as this one depicted in the Luttrell Psalter of about 1340.

39

DEATH OF A KNIGHT

In 1360 the Earl of Oxford died and the knight visited his castle, to pay his respects to the old earl's nephew, the new earl. Now the knight is feeling his age. He has seen great dangers, including the death of a third of the English population in the Black Death. Mercifully he survived, and finally dies peacefully in 1379, aged 60. This is not an unusual lifespan for someone of his rank and background. Peasants die much younger, because of poor diet and living conditions.

Knights queue to pledge fealty (allegiance) to a new overlord, in this case a king.

A knight's tomb

The knight is buried inside the local church, in a stone sepulchre (a stone box above the ground). On top of the tomb is an effigy carved in the latest fashion, a stone sculpture representing the knight in his armour. He looks relaxed, his legs crossed – as this is the current fashion in effigies – one hand on his sword and his feet resting on a lion.

The tomb is carved with his coat-of-arms and with some 'weepers', small figures, which might be family members, angels or saints, representing mourners. The tomb is a reminder to everyone who sees it how brave he was and how important his family is.

In the 1300s gunpowder arrived into Europe from China, and with it came the use of the cannon. The English first used cannon against the Scots, and against the French at the Siege of Calais in 1346.

Sir Thomas Malory, a knight, wrote *Le Morte D'Arthur* in 1470. Here are the last words of the dying King Arthur, as he drifts away on a magical boat to the blessed Isle of Avalon:

❖ *I will into the vale of Avalon to heal me of my grievous wound; and if thou hear no more of me, pray for my soul.* ❖

A knight's funeral could be a grand but solemn affair.

A new coat-of-arms

The knight's family are lucky. One of his sons has survived long enough to inherit his lands and title. His son uses the family coat-of-arms but adds a new symbol of his own. The knight's daughter can combine the coat-of-arms with her husband's coat-of-arms when she marries. If the knight had left no sons, his inheritance could have gone to his daughter if the earl allowed it. The family continue to owe allegiance to the earl, just as their father did before them.

The end of the fighting knights

The age of the fighting knights will soon be over. A line of charging knights is no match for a line of powerful long-range longbows or the cannon which will be used more and more in battle. By 1500 the knight's descendants will no longer go to fight for their lord. Instead, the king will use a professional army, and the knights will become local gentry concentrating on managing their estates. But the legends surrounding the knights of medieval times will survive for many centuries to come. When the knight was young he was inspired by tales of King Arthur's knights, and those myths will still be told hundreds of years later, keeping the idea of the chivalrous knight alive.

GLOSSARY

Archer ❖ a soldier trained to fire arrows from a bow

Betrothal ❖ a marriage arrangement, when young people are promised to each other in marriage

Black Death ❖ the name given to the disease that ravaged Europe in the late 1340s

Breech ❖ a hole smashed in the wall of a castle by a besieging enemy

Caparison ❖ a cloth coat worn by a medieval warhorse

Chain mail ❖ armour made from interlocking metal rings

Chevauchée ❖ a rampage by a medieval army through enemy country, to devastate farms and crops, and kill people

Chivalry ❖ a code of honourable behaviour for knights

Coat-of-arms ❖ the official badge of a noble family

Cross-guard ❖ the handle that goes across the top of a sword

Crusades ❖ a series of religious wars fought in medieval times, between Christian and Islamic forces, for control of Jerusalem. The city is revered as a holy place in both religions

Destrier ❖ a medieval warhorse

Dubbing ❖ the ceremony of a knight making someone else a knight by tapping their shoulders with a sword

Fealty ❖ loyalty to somebody, sealed with an oath. Another word for 'fealty' is 'allegiance'

Flail ❖ a metal ball on the end of a chain fixed to a wooden shaft — used as a weapon for crushing armour

Gatehouse ❖ the entrance to a big property such as a manor or a castle

Great Hall ❖ the large main room in a castle or manor, where meetings were held and meals eaten

Heir ❖ someone who is first in line to get land, goods, and perhaps a noble title passed down to them on their parents' death

Heraldry ❖ the official record of different coats-of-arms (badges identifying different noble families)

Holy Roman Empire ❖ a medieval kingdom stretching over central Europe, Germany and Italy

Inheritance ❖ land, money and sometimes a noble title handed on by a relative when they die — the oldest son was always first in line to inherit everything

Joust ❖ a tournament where two knights rode towards each other and scored points by striking their opponent with a lance

Knights Templar ❖ a group of religious knights who fought in the crusades during the 12th century

Lance ❖ a long metal pole with a sharp point, fixed to a wooden shaft

Mace ❖ a metal ball nailed to a wooden shaft and used as a weapon

Norman ❖ something or someone connected to the French forces that invaded England in 1066, led by William the Conqueror from Normandy. For instance, a castle described as 'Norman' means it was built by the invaders

Page ❖ a young boy aged seven or more, who served a knight and his family, while learning to be a knight

Pilgrimage ❖ a trip to a holy shrine

Plundering ❖ stealing goods and money from conquered people during an invasion

Portcullis ❖ the fortified entrance gate of a castle. It slid up and down over the entrance

Quarter ❖ mercy given to conquered soldiers by a victorious force — (to 'give no quarter' means to give no mercy)

Quintain ❖ a wooden training aid used for improving a knight's lance-aim. It had a shield on one side and a heavy sack on the other side which would hit a knight if he missed the shield

Ramparts ❖ the walkways around the tops of castle walls

Ransom ❖ a sum of money paid to release a hostage from captivity.

Reeve ❖ a knight's personal tax-collector

Relic ❖ a religious object connected to a saint

Retinue ❖ a group of knights who personally guarded a noble

Scabbard ❖ a sword-holder, made out of leather in medieval times

Siege tower ❖ a wooden tower with ladders on each side, rolled up to the wall of a castle for invading soldiers to climb up

Skirmish ❖ a fight between two enemy groups, smaller than a full-scale battle

Solar ❖ a private family room above the Great Hall in a castle or manor

Squire ❖ a young man (aged 14) who served a knight and was training to be a knight himself

Steward ❖ a knight's household assistant, who helped him manage his estate

Surcoat ❖ a tunic worn by a knight on top of his armour

Swaddling ❖ the bandages tightly wrapped around a medieval baby

Tenant ❖ someone who rents land or property belonging to somebody else

Trebuchet ❖ a giant wooden catapult, used to sling missiles at a castle during a siege

Vigil ❖ a long session of prayer, lasting for many hours. A squire held a vigil the night before he became a knight

Wet-nurse ❖ a woman paid to breast-feed another woman's baby

42

www.fordham.edu/halsall/sbook.html
A website where you can read many original documents.

www.mnsu.edu/emuseum/history/middleages/
A website where you can focus on life as a medieval peasant, knight, nun or merchant.

www.trytel.com
A website that provides historical information about cities and towns during the medieval period.

Note to parents and teachers:
Every effort has been made by the Publishers to ensure that the websites in this book are suitable for children, that they are of the highest educational value, and that they contain no inappropriate or offensive material. However, because of the nature of the Internet, it is impossible to guarantee that the contents of these sites will not be altered. We strongly advise that Internet access is supervised by a responsible adult.

TIMELINE

c.1000	over the next 200 years the European population grows enormously
1000	tournaments take place for the first time
1050	knights begin to charge with lances
1066	William of Normandy invades England – and is crowned King
1096	the first Crusade begins
c.1100	over the next 200 years, there is a great expansion of peasant settlement in Europe
c.1100	gradual introduction of the 'three-field' agricultural system across much of northern Europe
1135–54	civil war in England
1146–1254	further crusades - 2nd to 7th
1150	knights start to use coats-of-arms
1200	knights start to put armour on their horses
c.1200	some peasant houses are being built of stone in northern Europe
c.1200	German peasant houses begin to introduce a smokeless stove (stube) to heat their homes
c.1200	horses replace cattle to pull heavy loads in northern Europe
c.1200	money rents gradually replace labour services – growth of towns, trade and the money economy
1205	the River Thames freezes and can be crossed over the ice
1207	the Order of St Francis is formed in Italy
1208	King John quarrels with the Pope, who bans church services in England
1215	King John signs the Magna Carta, giving the nobles more power
1252	Henry III is given a polar bear, which swims in the River Thames with a muzzle and chain
1260	the cathedral is consecrated at Chartres in France
1265	Marco Polo travels to the Far East
c.1270	the oldest paper manufacturing in Christian Europe at Fabriano, Italy
1279	new silver coins created in England – the groat (4d), a round farthing and a halfpenny
1285	spectacles are made in northern Italy
c.1310	the mechanical clock is perfected
1317	heavy rains and ruined harvests cause famine across Europe
1327	the murder of Edward II
1323–28	peasant revolts in the Netherlands
1337	the outbreak of the Hundred Years' War between England and France
1344	the first English gold coin, the noble, is worth 6s 8d
1346	the Battle of Crécy – early cannon are used, as well as longbows
1348-49	the arrival of the bubonic plague, 'Black Death', in Europe
1361	plague breaks out again
1362	William Langland begins to write his poem, *Piers Plowman*
1369	harvests fail across Europe
1381	the Peasants' Revolt in England
1387	Geoffrey Chaucer begins his *Canterbury Tales*
1388	the first town sanitation act is passed in the English parliament
1437–38	ruined harvests, famine and plague occur in many parts of Europe
1438–40	heavy rains and ruined harvests in England
1430–70	economic crises hit England – many peasants are ruined
1453	the end of the Hundred Years War between England and France
1470	an economic revival begins

INDEX

These are the lists of contents for each title in *Medieval Lives*:

Peasant

Introduction · First years · Peasant cottage · Childhood
The Church · Marriage · Land · Work-service for the manor · The manorial court
The working year · Feeding the family · Sickness and health · Women's work · Earning money
Games and entertainment · Freedom · Last days · Glossary · Timeline/Useful websites · Index

Merchant

Introduction · First days · House and home · Growing up · School · Becoming a merchant
Marriage · The wool trade · Travel and communication · War and piracy · Secrets of success
Branching out · Wealth and property · The merchant's wife · Good works · Health and diet
The end · Glossary · Timeline/Useful websites · Index

Knight

All about knights · A future knight is born · Time to leave home · Becoming a squire
A squire goes forth · Becoming a knight · Invitation to the castle · Joust! · Called to war
Battlefield tactics · Dressed to kill · Weapons · Siege warfare · Pilgrimage · Returning home
Knightly duties · Death of a knight · Glossary · Timeline/Useful websites · Index

Nun

Introduction · Birth · Childhood and education · To the nunnery – postulant
The nunnery itself · Taking the veil – novice · Daily life – the offices · The inner life
Daily routine · Enclosure · Cellaress and librarian · The world outside · Priests and nuns
Poverty and personal possessions · A visitation · Difficult times · Death · Glossary
Timeline/Useful websites · Index

Lady of the Manor

A medieval lady · A lady is born · Invitation to a wedding
At home with a lady · Wifely duties · Noble children · A year in the life
Clothes and hairstyles · A lady's hobbies · A lady's books · Time to eat · The lady falls ill
Women who work · The noblest ladies · A visit to a nunnery · The world outside
Widowhood · Glossary · Timeline/Useful websites · Index

Stonemason

Introduction · Birth · Childhood and growing up · Training - the quarry
Training - the building site · Rough-mason – a bridge · Summoned to work - a castle
A real 'mason' - the abbey · A growing reputation · Stone-carver · The lodge
Under-mason for the college · Master-mason for the cathedral · Designing the cathedral
Building the cathedral · Retirement · End of a life · Glossary · Timeline/Useful websites · Index